CHANGE

GETTING TO KNOW ABOUT EBB AND FLOW

by Laura Greene

illustrated by Gretchen Mayo

Printed in the United States of America.
9876543210 — 987654321

Library of Congress Cataloging in Publication Data

Greene, Laura.
Change: Getting to know about ebb and flow.

SUMMARY: Explains that changes, both good and bad, are a constant part of life.

1. Social change—Juvenile literature. 2. Personality change—Juvenile literature. 3. Change—Juvenile literature. (1. Change) I. Mayo, Gretchen. II. Title.

HM101.G82   303.4   80-81081
ISBN-0-87705-401-0

For my mother, Ida Katz Offenhartz

Change is a part of life.
It is a step from here to there.
The size or shape of a thing may change.
The feeling or location of a thing may change.
Change may be fast or slow, good or bad.
Change may make me happier or sadder,
richer or poorer, but change
is a part of life.

All things in nature change.

Things change with time.
Time brings slow change.

In time seeds grow,

and become plants.

More time passes and the plants become flowers.

Time continues to pass
and the flowers
fade,
die
and finally return
to earth.

Seasons change.

When the air is warm, the leaves are green.
When the air turns cold, the leaves turn color.

The sun makes the difference.

Shadows change.

In the morning my shadow is long and skinny.
At midday my shadow is short and fat.

Light makes the difference.

Sounds change.

Sometimes the air is so quiet, I can hear a bird fly.
Sometimes the air is so noisy, I can't hear a bird sing.

Wind makes the difference.

Things change because of accidents.

The accident may be little.

I had a full glass of milk.
In a moment the glass was empty.
My elbow made the difference.

The accident may be big.

Yesterday there was a white house on the corner.
Today it's gone.

A fire made the difference.

People change too.

They change on the outside . . . .

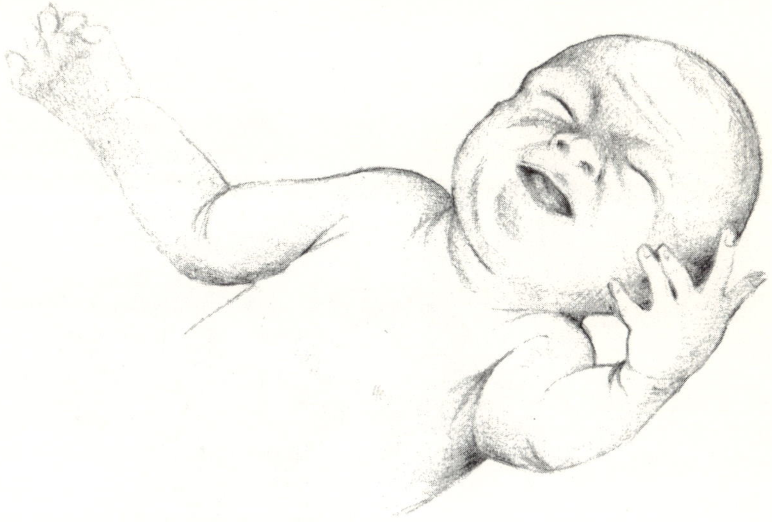

My skin changes.
When I was a baby, my skin was red and wrinkled.
Now my skin is smooth.
When I grow older, I'll be wrinkled again.

Age makes the difference.

My height changes.

When my jeans were new, they were much too long.
Now they're old and much too short.

Growing makes the difference.

. . . . and people change on the inside.

Feelings change.

I used to be afraid to go to school.
But now I'm not, in fact, I like it.

Learning makes the difference.

Moods change.

It's fun to be alone in my room and pretend
to do great deeds.
But if I'm alone at night, and there are scary
shadows, it's not fun any more.

The dark makes the difference.

Tastes change.

Tuna fish sandwiches used to be my favorite lunch.
But now I like macaroni and cheese better.

I don't know what made the difference.

People cause change.

We change each other . . .

When I moved away, my friend Jenny was sad.
She missed me.
But now we're pen pals, and she's happy.

Friendship made the difference.

We change the land.

I can make land more beautiful by planting a tree
or I can ruin the land by being careless.

All of us make the difference.

People change themselves.

If I want to, I can work hard and learn to do things better.

If I don't want to try new things, I'll stay the same.

I make the difference.

Life around us is always changing.

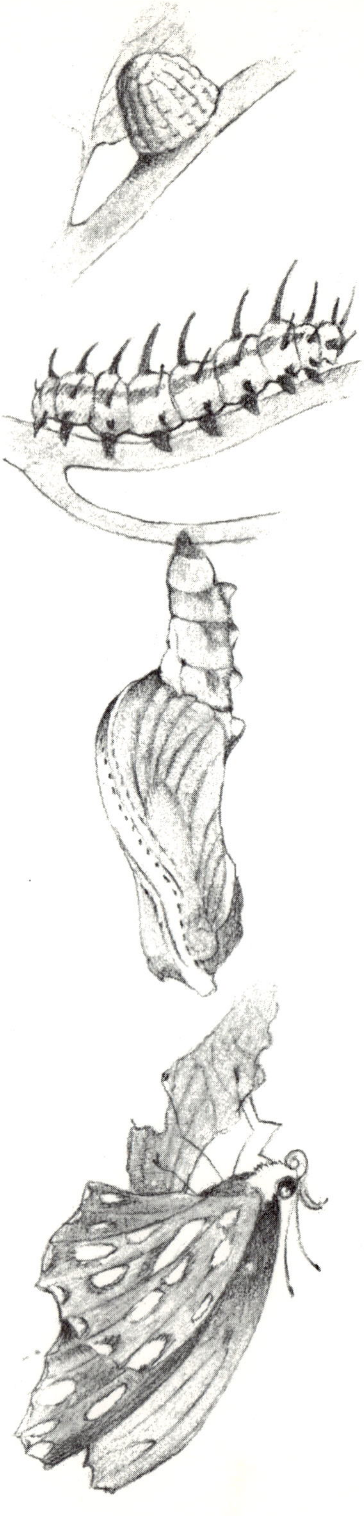

Change is part of life.

Sometimes I like the change.

Sometimes I don't.

But everything changes.

Even me!